READY TO GIVE AN ANSWER

READY TO GIVE AN ANSWER

Kim Darnell

Join my email list to STAY IN TOUCH and
receive a FREE PDF of Questions for Reflection!

https://mailchi.mp/4ad9d5f2280d/kimdarnell

Table of Contents

For my loved ones

INTRODUCTION

....

"But in your hearts revere Christ as Lord. Always be prepared to give an answer to everyone who asks you to give the reason for the hope that you have." ~1 Peter 3:15

1 Peter 3:15 is one of those verses that I recognize as important, worthy of being underlined in my Bible and of enthusiastic agreement when it comes up in church. But it is also one of those verses that has troubled me many times. If someone were to actually ask me why I have hope in Christ, what would be my answer?

As someone who knows and loves many nonbelievers, this challenge to have my response ready feels pressing but can also feel pointless. It's not like many people just come up asking me about my faith. They know, or they assume they know, what I believe. They know that I'm a Christian. But do they know why? Do I?

KIM DARNELL

The more I allowed myself to contemplate this, the more I realized how important it was that I articulate my answer. Not just for someone who may or may not ask, but for myself. I once read that most people in America today are not atheists or agnostics or Christians, but ex-Christians. People who once identified themselves as believers but who no longer do. Many of them don't make that decision in one life-altering moment. They simply drift away from faith.

I've seen it. I've watched several friends from youth group go from being so passionate about standing out in their faith to taking small breaks from the Christian world to being indifferent or even hostile towards God. This is a fact that burdens me to my core, a devastation that I never want to be part of my story. So I set out to refine my answer, to pinpoint the reason I've put my hope in God. For me, for something to hold on to in moments of trial, and for others, for the genuine response that they deserve from someone who claims to have such a life-changing hope.

If you want to skip the book, and just know my answer, I would be okay with that. Because I am ready to give an answer, and I want the world to hear it! Writing it down as a belief statement in bold ink is the best way the writer inside of me knows how to express it.

The reason I have hope in Jesus is because I have experienced Him as the way and the truth and the life.

"How?" you ask, or "What does that mean?" Well if you want to know that, then I suppose you won't be skipping the book. This book is going to showcase what that experience has looked like for me personally—from a young child who learned that Jesus offers a better way of life than alcoholism or wildness, to a young adult who struggled with identity crises and found that He also offers truth too rich to fathom, and finally to an older adult who is daily discovering what it is to have a full, abundant life that is certainly not devoid of troubles and temptations but that is nevertheless filled with joy and purpose.

If you're reading this and you haven't experienced that, I pray that God would open your eyes to Him and His love, and that you would seek that as you read my account. Jesus isn't just the way and the truth and the life for me. He is that and so much more for all who choose to believe in Him.

If you're reading this as a fellow believer, I hope my testimony encourages you in your faith. May it challenge you to consider your own journey, to be ready to give your own answer.

"Jesus answered, 'I am the way and the truth and the life. No one comes to the Father except through me.'" ~John 14:6

PART I: THE WAY

I don't remember the day I got saved. Many people have amazing salvation stories—they witnessed a miracle or they were overtaken by a revelation of God's love that brought them to tears. And then there are those who don't remember the day they got saved because they grew up in church and just can't pinpoint the exact date. My story's not like that either.

Jesus wasn't someone I grew up knowing or taking for granted, and He wasn't someone I met in a magical instant, but rather someone who revealed Himself to me a little at a time, like a distant father visiting as much as a confused child will allow, patiently gaining my trust.

***

"God bless mommy and daddy and Melissa and Amelia and Sandi and Kimi and all those less fortunate than us...." My dad used to pray those words with me almost every night, a faithful petition for our family of six, a family that often felt a bit strained. Finishing his prayer, my dad would kiss me on the forehead and say good night, and as he bent over me, I would smell the traces of alcohol on his breath.

My dad was not an abusive alcoholic. He was a contemplative one. He would drink beer after beer almost every night when he got home from work, often out in the garage, staring out the window into the horizon. Sometimes he would put on music in the living room and play with his old drumsticks with a giddy smile on his face. Other times he would sit fragilely at the kitchen table with tears streaming down his face as he listened to "Cats in the Cradle" and other songs that reminded him of his late father.

The whole family would be left pleading with him on school nights to *please turn off the music because we all need to go to sleep.* He would answer, "Just a couple more." Then, when pressed twenty or thirty minutes later, it would seem that he'd never heard our first request nor that he was registering our present one, he was in such a world of his own, bobbing his head to the music and searching his collection of cassettes for his next pick.

My sisters and I felt like we had no relationship with dad. He did his own thing, and we did ours. I was the one who got the most face time with him because I liked to ride his shiny blue Harley Sportster with him. During the summertime, we would take short day trips on the motorcycle, making frequent stops at gas stations to stretch our legs and sit outside. My dad would always ask, "You want a Big Jim?" which really meant a "Big Ed" ice cream sandwich. Of course, he would come out of the store with a 32oz can of Bud Light as well, and we would sit together until my fingers were sticky with ice cream and his beer and cigarettes ran out.

At school, I learned of the dangers of drinking and driving, and I remember asking my dad once if he would not drink when we were out on motorcycle rides. Before we left the house for our ride one Saturday morning, I had him promise me that he wouldn't. About ten minutes later, we stopped at our local gas station to fill up before we headed out of town, and he came out of the store with a brown bag. My heart sank. "You said you wouldn't," I said pitifully. He didn't say anything as he popped the can open and took a big swallow. He didn't even look at me.

The day my dad called a "family meeting," my three sisters and I were all confused, since family meetings were not exactly a familiar concept in our home. At our mother's prodding, we gathered around the kitchen table, our round faces looking up at him, noticing his distress. He was silent for a moment before he started to struggle to get his words out between sobs.

"It's a disease," I remember him saying, as he stood clutching his chair with one hand and wiping his tears with another. Something called alcoholism, an addiction that had caused him to miss out on so much of our family's life. He was going to try to get help.

As a young child, I may or may not have understood all that was being said, but I remember tears coming to my own eyes as I watched his display of sorrow. And I will always look back on it as my first lesson on repentance—that it is difficult and necessary and good all at the same time.

***

Since my dad was somewhat absent in our childhood and my mom was not cut out to be a disciplinarian, my sisters and I were left with a lot of freedom growing up. For the most part, this involved a lot of boys and experimentation with all things "cool" and wild. Our ages are like an evenly spaced ladder, where Mese is the oldest at the top, two years down is Maya, another couple years down is Sandi, and another two years down at the bottom is me. Being the youngest, I looked at their lives as the norm that I should follow and watched each one develop a similar lifestyle: They had boyfriends, partied, and had strokes of rebellion against our parents—pretty typical adolescent behavior. But as a child, seeing Maya throwing up in the toilet after drinking too much or watching the distress of Sandi's boyfriend after a difficult breakup–those things really troubled my young heart.

I remember taking a swig of a drink and a puff of a cigarette in elementary school. I had my first boyfriend in second grade. But I recognized early on that those things were let-downs. I felt more alive searching my heart to write poetry than I did doing anything else. And all I knew in all that soul-searching was that I was surrounded by a way of life that didn't appeal to me, and I longed for something more.

By the time I got to junior high, my perceptiveness must have been clear to my parents because one night, I remember overhearing a heated argument between them and Maya and her boyfriend. My dad was saying how he didn't want me seeing her boyfriend staying the night all the time and hearing the things that were going on in her room. Maya cried like it was the end of the world and swore her and Andy would move out together. And, several months later, they did.

I cried over boys, too, and longed for young love. That was the only thing I saw being of deeper value than all of the other shenanigans I witnessed. It made people *feel*—whether happy or sad or angry, it was something that people really seemed to care about.

In sixth grade, I had a boyfriend named Victor whom I adored. We used to meet outside of our classroom at the end of each day and give each other a peck on the lips. I only remember going to his house once and feeling so embarrassed to even eat in front of him that by the end of our "date" my stomach hurt from being so worked up.

7

When he moved away and the inevitable breakup happened, I wrote my first love poem. I remember swinging in our hammock in the backyard and allowing the tears to trickle down my cheeks as I put my melodramatic feelings to paper. That event repeated itself a few times throughout my adolescent years: me writing about love, trying to figure out just what it was. Me reaching for it again and again because I knew it was the best thing I'd seen yet. And me being ever confused and disappointed by it because it would never be enough.

***

When I was in junior high, my sister Sandi was dating a boy named Hunter. He was a tall, goofy guy with dark hair and a great smile. He always had a surplus of energy and was very sociable. But if he had to be defined by one word, it would be sweet. He just had one of those kind dispositions that always aimed to please others. And since he was head over heels for my sister, the main person he wanted to please was her.

They were always together. They spoke in kiddy voices to each other. He made a habit of bringing her small gifts, even if it was just a bottle of Sobe (her favorite drink at the time). To me, it was true love, and I was fascinated by it.

I loved hanging out with them. I would linger in the living room to play car racing video games or watch movies with them. I would tag

8

along on car rides, where we'd blast Jimmy Eat World and Hunter would sing out the words and squeeze my sister's hand, trying to get her to smile.

Sandi and I shared a room, and one day I was in there by myself crying over some boy. Hunter walked in looking for Sandi, but when he saw me, a look of concern washed over his face and he stopped to ask me what was wrong. With new tears brimming in my eyes, I told him that I had been dumped.

I don't have a brother, but I imagine he responded the way a very kind brother would have. He opened his arms and hugged me and told me that the boy was stupid and I was beautiful. I will never forget how special that made me feel, that someone who knew so much about being in love thought I was worthy of it.

It was my heart that broke the day that Hunter and Sandi split up. I had never seen a guy so upset, his eyes red from crying, his voice strained, sobs still catching in his throat as he hurried out the door to his car. I remember crying myself as I worried about him driving away like that, wondering why Sandi had rejected someone who loved her so much. I know now that relationships are complicated and that those two young high schoolers probably weren't meant to be together forever. And I know now that it is not always easy for people to accept someone's love.

***

My high school sweetheart was a hefty boy with brown hair, a wide nose, and teeth that stuck out at you when he spoke (which was often because he was quite the storyteller). A lot of people didn't understand my attraction, but I hardly noticed his disheveled appearance. It was his heart that I fell in love with, and his enthusiasm for life. He was just a carefree kind of guy, and I liked how it balanced out my somewhat high-strung nature. He was fun, and he brought out the fun side of me. Plus, he adored me.

When we spent time together, we would usually ride dirt bikes or listen to hard rock, picking out all of the lyrics we liked best. But one night when he invited me over, I showed up to find that David had a couple of friends over and they had all been drinking. It was completely unexpected since he hadn't mentioned anything about drinking being something he was into, so I felt surprised— deceived, even. David was stumbling over his words thinking everything was so funny, but to me he was not nearly as funny as he usually was without alcohol. When he realized I was uncomfortable, he kept apologizing and trying to put his arm around me, not seeming to notice that I kept inching away from him, not wanting to be touched. The smell of alcohol in the room and the way he was not acting like himself really bothered me, and I told him I wanted to leave.

I hadn't been gone long, so when I got home, my mom called to me from the kitchen saying, "That was quick." All I had to do was look at her for her to know that I was upset. My mom gives the best hugs, and as my body fell into hers, the tears came.

"Kimi, what's the matter?" she asked as she stroked my hair back with one hand and held me close with the other. I don't remember the words I used to tell her that David was drunk but I remember the words I ended with that made my mom cry, too: "I don't want to be with someone like Dad."

After a brief silence, my mom said something about love and how change takes time, but I hardly heard her response, I felt so awful about what I'd said.

I didn't know it then, but the truth was that it had nothing to do with my dad. I had the same feeling of distaste several months later when David and I were kissing and he put my hand somewhere I wasn't comfortable with, and again when he told me he smoked weed. It was a sense that there had to be a reason behind my conscience, that there had to be more to life.

Later I would find that C.S. Lewis said it better than I ever could: "It would seem that Our Lord finds our desires not too strong, but too weak. We are half-hearted creatures, fooling about with drink and sex and ambition when

11

infinite joy is offered us, like an ignorant child who wants to go on making mud pies in a slum because he cannot imagine what is meant by the offer of a holiday at the sea. We are far too easily pleased."[1]

***

To this day, my parents and sisters are some of the closest people to my heart. My dad's turnaround inspires me, as does my mom's unyielding patience and faith as she has stood by him through his alcoholism and recovery. My sisters have given me friendship and been some of my biggest cheerleaders through life. But as with most, my family has also shown me that everyone falls short, makes mistakes, gets lost. I hear others' stories of growing up in seemingly perfect Christian homes, and while part of me wishes I could name all the books of the Bible by heart and that my sisters and I could sing all of the VeggieTales songs together, I am truly thankful that I grew up knowing a need for a Savior.

I felt that need greatly on the day I rushed to the hospital with my oldest sister Mese after she had made an attempt on her own life. After finding several empty sleeping pill casings in the bathroom trash, my parents had frantically run into her bedroom to try to wake her up. She

---

[1] C.S. Lewis, *The Weight of Glory and Other Addresses* (New York: HarperCollins, 1949; reprint, 2001), 26.

couldn't quite come to, but she was conscious enough to drag her feet and lean on their shoulders as they rushed her to the car.

After we admitted her at the hospital, we weren't allowed to see her until she was stabilized. When they let us into the room, she was still sleeping. She had an IV attached to her wrist and some spit-up on her hospital bib. I remember that detail most clearly of all. Perhaps I was searching for something simple to focus on in the face of something so incomprehensible.

We were all gathered next to her bedside, my dad wearing a sullen expression with a wrinkled brow, and my mom silently wiping tears from her cheeks. I remember taking hold of Mese's limp hand and feeling the weight of its lifelessness. She was already a thin girl, but she looked especially so in that moment. Her lips were pale, nearly blending in to her fair skin. I don't think it was until my dad backed away into a corner and broke the silence with his uncontrollable sobs that the gravity of the situation hit me. Sorrow descended like a 50 pound crowbar on my shoulders, making my whole body and spirit feel strained. My sister was alive, but not full of life.

As I sat there, I knew that life was better than death, that life was worth living—even if I didn't quite know why.

***

It was when I started going to youth group that I felt it click. My sister Sandi had started attending and decided to bring me along.

Wednesday night services were held in the gym of the church. Anywhere from twenty to fifty junior high and high school age students would show up each week. The services would typically start with an outrageous icebreaker or game to get everyone out of their seats and having fun (hey, not everyone can say they've won a Spam-eating contest!). Then, there was a worship band comprised of mostly high-schoolers that would play upbeat worship music, then transition to slower, more meaningful songs about how Jesus was worth living for. The words would be up on a projector screen so that everyone could sing along. Finally, our youth pastor would get up and introduce that week's topic, then lay out several different Bible verses and life stories that showed what God had to say about it, encouraging us to follow along in our own Bibles. He would talk about anything from the importance of prayer and reading the Bible to how to date wisely.

I saw everyone singing with smiles on their faces and I heard the pastor speak with conviction about a way of life that appealed so much more to me—where purity and wisdom were sought after, rather than the temporary highs with which everyone else was so overtaken. I felt a joy that I had never before experienced as I learned more about the sacrificial love of Jesus and His higher plan. For me. For my loved ones. For everyone, everywhere.

I had known about God before, had prayed, had even been baptized of my own choice, but it wasn't until I was surrounded by so many other young people pouring their hearts out to someone personal that I realized Jesus wasn't just there to believe in, but to love. I was overtaken by his goodness and calling to be set apart from a fallen world. My disenchantment with society's way of life met an enchantment with Jesus' way of life. And thus my journey of faith began.

***

I didn't always get it right when it came to living God's way. That couldn't be truer than when it came to my social decisions in high school.

Since I was so involved in youth group, I made a lot of Christian friends. I did have a couple of friends who were not believers that I would hang out with outside of school, including my friend Jess, who I had known since grade school. The problem was, the further I moved into my faith in God, the further she seemed to move away from it, and she started to make me feel challenged and on edge every time we spent time together. Her questions about my faith and the shame I felt when I made mistakes in front of her didn't

15

make for very friendly experiences, and I started to dread spending time with her.

One day, as we were driving in the car together, I told her that maybe we shouldn't be friends anymore because it didn't seem like we had much in common. I essentially broke up with her using that as my reason instead of simply telling her how I felt and learning how to wrestle with my perfectionism and ignorance. And of course, she was hurt and angry. She knew that it had to do with my faith, but neither of us knew I was just too spiritually immature to love her the way I should have.

Of course, this had a snowball effect, and a mutual friend decided she couldn't be friends with me any more either if that's "the type of person I was." My apologies and appeals had little effect because they were not followed by the actions of acceptance and love that they were both looking for.

I will always regret the way I handled that situation, and I admit that I am a flawed "type of person" and that I will never be able to apologize enough for the times I've shown others such a lesser version of who God is. But that's why God's grace is so beautiful. His way says I won't always get it right, but I can always find forgiveness and hope in Him. Hope that I won't repeat mistakes and hope that those I've hurt will still be able to know His love.

***

I was once at a Christian gathering where the leaders had the teens they'd been ministering to come up and share about how their lives had changed since meeting Jesus. Each teen had a poster board with their "name" or identity before meeting Christ on one side, and their name after meeting Christ on the other. One teen mom shared her "before" identity as "a statistic" then flipped over the board with tears in her eyes proudly proclaiming that she was now "a one of a kind mom and future chef." Another shared that he'd gone from "pathetic" to "worthy." I thought it was such a beautiful way to honor what God had done in their lives, and I got to thinking about what I would have said if I were asked to sum up in just a few words how Jesus had changed the way I viewed myself.

I think my "before" identity would be *Seeker.* I was searching for purpose from as early as I can remember. I didn't have clear beliefs about the world or God or myself, so I was left bumbling around, grasping at various things, testing them for meaning.

I found meaning when I realized that I have a Heavenly Father who loves me and shows me how life works best. So the "after" identity I found was this: *Child of God.*

I am a daughter following in her Dad's footsteps as He leads the way.

17

PART II: THE TRUTH

"Okay, I love you too." There was no trace of sincerity on my lips. I practically pushed my parents away. I watched the tears roll down my mom's cheeks and the corrected posture of my dad as he strained not to break down himself, and I couldn't muster one ounce of grief for them. They had flown to Minneapolis with me from our small hometown in Northern California to drop me off at the private university I'd selected, and we had spent the last few days together touring the area and "bonding." I don't know if it was the strain of having to say goodbye to all of my friends, the lasting effects of jet lag, or my sheer impatience with my parents at a time when I just wanted to be on my own already, but I was nothing but irritable the entire trip. Now, as the time was finally coming to a close, I was more anxious than ever to be rid of them so that my college experience could really start.

"Bye," I said and watched them walk out the front doors of my new school, my new home. I sighed. It was initially a sigh of relief to be free of their presence and gloom, but towards the end, my breath wavered. As I turned and walked down the hall by myself, my face grew hot and I did what I couldn't do just thirty seconds before. I cried. I wanted another one of my mom's hugs. I wanted to say I was sorry for treating her and Dad so horribly. I called them as I walked back to my dorm room.

"Mom," I cried into the phone, "I'm sorry." She and my dad got the sincere, "I love you's" that they had been yearning for, and they seemed to understand my emotional fluctuation. I hung up the phone feeling better but not good. I assumed this would wear off shortly. I was wrong.

***

I wasn't entirely by myself at North Central University. My high school sweetheart David had enrolled there as well, and he arrived shortly after my parents' departure. Yes, this is the same David who pushed me to the edge of my comfort zone several times in high school, but when he met Jesus, he became someone who cared deeply about people and about pleasing God. Every time I looked at him, I saw what God must have been talking about when he called the David of the Bible "a man after His own heart." He was not perfect, but he was burdened by his failures and passionate about loving God and others.

All of our friends wanted what we had. I can't count the times I heard people from our youth group who were trying to get involved with a significant other say, "I just want to be like Kim and David."

It was because we were amiable. We weren't the type of couple that people felt out of place with because we enjoyed always being with our friends. At the same time, we didn't mask our feelings for each other and were obviously in love. We would fully devote our attention to the people around us yet still allow for tender moments– a long gaze into each other's eyes, a pet name, his moving my hair behind my ear or tracing my hand with his fingers.

We were the token couple in our youth group. Well, we had been. That summer, we had declared that we were on "a break" to make sure that our priorities were in the right place before embarking on this huge change. This wasn't the first time we'd done this. We had every intention of getting back together, but for some reason, we hadn't yet. And I was okay with that. Late in the summer, I had entertained a two-week romance with one of my longtime friends, and although we had agreed to do nothing about it, I wasn't sure I was ready to be official with David again. The hometown crush had opened my mind to the idea that there were lots of possible prospects out there, and maybe it wouldn't be a bad idea to be open to the thought that "the one" could be someone other than David. Of course, this was all thought subconsciously.

In my young, naive mind I was going to marry David. We'd talked about it and everything. In fact, we'd wanted to get married before school even started but had no possible means of making that a reality, and so had left the idea hanging. But it was still very much an idea.

For years we had been inseparable. There weren't many times that you'd hear one name without the other. "Where're Kim and David?" "What are Kim and David doing?" "We should invite Kim and David!" It's strange to think about how swiftly that changed.

There were signs, sure enough. Of course, there was the separation during the summer where we didn't spend nearly as much time together as we usually did. I thought that would change when we got to this big, scary place where we were the only person the other one knew. But it didn't.

Sure, we hung out. We explored the campus and the nearby shops together, and we met to eat or talk fairly often. It must have been more often than I realized actually because people were always asking if we were an item.

"What are you up to?" a new friend of ours asked me one evening as I stood by the elevators in the lobby.

"Just waiting for David," I replied.

"What's up with you guys anyway?" he asked. I pretended not to know what he meant. "You guys are always together," he prodded. "But you're not a couple?"

"Nope," I said coolly, thinking that was the most accurate answer for the time being. "We used to be, but we're just friends right now."

24

"You guys have the weirdest relationship I've ever heard of," he commented as he shook his head lightly and went on his way.

***

We both made new friends rather rapidly. North Central was a small Christian school, and within weeks it seemed like everybody knew everybody. There were events thrown for people of the same major, floor activities, school-wide events, and a number of different ministry groups that you could join based on your interests. This was on top of the people you met in classes or in chapel services (which everyone was required to go to on a daily basis). So neither David nor I were ever at a loss for company. It felt natural that we didn't spend all our time together since we were immersed in groups of other people.

However, it didn't take long for me to feel out of place among the people in my major. I had chosen Intercultural Studies (ICS)—David and I both had. We wanted to be missionaries. But my lack of enthusiasm for other cultures started to make me uncomfortable. The very first time that all of the ICS first-years got together to share, this worry surfaced.

"Let's go around the room and share your name, a little bit about yourself, and what you want to do with your major," the facilitator announced. The first girl started.

"My name's Alyssa. I'm 18, and I'm from Wisconsin; that's where I grew up my whole life.... And I'm majoring in Intercultural Studies because I have always had a heart for the less fortunate in Africa. Their whole way of life is just fascinating to me, and I want to be able to give them the health care and the resources that they need, and of course, be able to witness to them about the Lord...." She went on from there, elaborating on her passion for what seemed like forever. The other majors had similarly detailed accounts of the area of the world that they were most enthralled with and how desperately they wanted to reach them. All I could think was that I wanted to minister to kids somewhere, but I wouldn't be caught saying something as informal as that. By the time my turn came, I was practically panicking.

"I... uh... Well, my name's Kim, and I'm from California... and I really have a heart for kids. I think I'll minister in South America because I have a pretty good knack for Spanish...." Everyone smiled and nodded, but I knew I sounded ridiculous. I didn't want to go to South America because I was in love with their culture or even aware of their needs; I wanted to go just because I thought I could handle the language! My face grew red, and my rambling came to a quick halt. "And yeah..." I trailed off with a nervous laugh.

Needless to say, I didn't go to many other ICS events, partly because I felt foolish and out of place, and partly because the events simply

26

weren't interesting to me. "Come experience the tastes of China!" a flyer would read, or "Please join us to watch a documentary on Egypt!" *I'd rather go out with my girlfriends,* I would think to myself. This made me certain that I needed to rethink my choice of major.

I started probing myself, asking questions like, *Well, what do I have to offer people? Do I just want to preach to random kids in foreign countries, or is there anything else I feel led to share?"* And I heard my heart saying, *Love, yes. The Gospel, yes....and education.*

It was a breakthrough thought for me. I was my high school valedictorian, and I had always not only been good at school, but actually enjoyed it. I loved learning. I had worked my senior year as a tutor, and I loved that, too. And that's when it clicked. I should be an Education major! I was good at teaching others, and I liked doing it! In fact, senior year I had also volunteered for Study Buddy, and the teacher I volunteered under had watched me working with her second-graders one day and commented, "You're a natural!" I had laughed it off at the time. The last thing I wanted to be was a teacher. But what if I turned education into my own mission field? My own way to minister to kids– kids who really needed it? The less fortunate, abandoned ones in third-world countries?

I was ecstatic to tack Elementary Education onto my Intercultural Studies focus. Sure, double-majoring would be hard, but it gave me a clear direction. Just a couple months later, that direction got narrowed even further. My boredom during my Global Perspectives class continually reinforced how little passion I had for foreign countries, and I decided to drop the ICS part altogether. I could help less fortunate kids here in the United States!

David was less than supportive. "What about the mission field?" he protested, thinking I had abandoned my calling when I was convinced I was merely focusing it. He had picked up a sudden interest in Muslim culture, and he was ready to pack his bags and minister in Iraq. This was yet another sign that "Kim and David" might not last forever.

If I had to choose a country to be passionate about, Iraq would probably be at the bottom of my list. It's just never been a land or a way of life that sparked my interest, and I didn't know how to respond when David told me that was where he wanted to serve. Either God was going to stage a major change of heart in me, or else a future with David was not going to work.

I started praying about it, hoping maybe David would change his mind. I was always reminded that it was out of my hands, and I didn't need to worry about it. So I didn't. Until it all came crashing down.

***

The day we did face it we were alone in my dorm room. We had been listening to music online—his favorite thing to do—but in a matter of moments, our casual hang-out session turned into a heart-wrenching breakup scene.

"Kim, I really feel like we're just supposed to be friends," he said as tears came to his eyes. "I think we're called to different things."

"I know," I said, at first relieved that we were finally addressing it. We hugged, and it felt like a load had been lifted.

And then, it didn't.

As he held me close to him and let his sobs break free, I felt myself grabbing onto him for dear life. It had been "Kim and David" for so long. I was supposed to marry him! Now it was sealed that was no longer an option, and I couldn't handle it. I was suddenly gripped by dread and grief, and I cried hard into his shoulder for what must have been half an hour.

I recovered long enough to properly say goodbye.

"You're still my best friend," he told me. "I don't want that to change."

"I don't either," I shook my head and let out a long breath. It was painful enough having him not be my boyfriend; there was no way I could manage his not being my friend, too.

He smiled weakly and walked out the door.

As it closed behind him, emptiness loomed over me. I broke down worse than I had ever broken down before. With loud cries, I let it all out for hours on my dorm floor. When I had finally got a hold of myself, I could hardly recognize my face in the mirror, my eyes were

29

so swollen and red, and that made me cry even more. It was the most devastating thing I had ever faced at that point in my life.

I had really believed that we were meant for each other. If that wasn't true, what else was I believing in that wasn't real?

***

That day changed me. I wasn't as joyful as usual. I was more homesick than I'd ever been. And it took a great toll on my faith. I felt like God was a liar, or else I was really bad at hearing from Him. I had been certain that He'd brought me and David together for a reason. How could He just change that? Was He punishing me?

I started feeling constantly ashamed before Him, so I didn't pray as much. This was in stark contrast to my formerly regimented devotional life. Every day in high school, I would wake up an hour and a half early so I could not only pray and read my Bible by myself but also arrive at school early enough to join my peers for corporate prayer at the flagpole before the first bell sounded. Now, I found myself relying on chapel services as my fuel for the day. God was constantly reminding me of his patience and love, but that just made me feel more distant from Him because I couldn't understand it. I wanted Him to reveal deeper things to me, like how I was supposed to carry on living for Him when I had no clue how

to do it now that I was on my own. Part of me
didn't even know if I wanted to live for Him
anymore.
I was embarrassed by my struggle, but I had
to talk to someone.
"Do you ever think about just doing
something crazy?" I confided to Kate, one of the
closest friends I'd made at North Central. "Ya
know, something bad?"
"Well sure. I think everyone does," she said
considerately. "I've been thinking about that a
lot myself lately."
"Really?" I hadn't expected her to
understand. Her sensitivity spurred me on. "I
just feel really unmotivated about my faith
lately. Like I'm getting so far away from God
and I don't even care."
"I know exactly what you mean."
I don't think any words could have given me
more encouragement. But the fact still
remained: we were struggling. Several days
later, I still had the urge to rebel.
"Ya know what we were talking about the
other day?" I brought it up somewhat
nervously. What if she'd resolved the issue for
herself and I was the only one still left with this
silly notion?
"Yeah?" she answered.
"Well... I think we should do something," I
said, half-embarrassed. "Would you be
interested in that?"
"Sure," she said. "I just don't know what we'd
do."

KIM DARNELL

Only a few ideas had crossed my mind, and
none of them sounded that appealing. The only
things I thought about suggesting were going to
a party or smoking a cigarette, and I couldn't
even bring myself to say those because the
whole thing sounded so childish out loud.
"I don't know either."
And that's as far as that stroke of rebellion
ever got.

***

Everyone imagines their first year away at
college to be amazing. It's the starting point of
freedom, independence, and excitement... isn't
it? Well I was free, in a sense, since I was now
living across the country from my parents; I
was independent enough (the loan for my
overpriced school was in my name, wasn't it?);
and there were some definite points of
excitement going out to concerts and pulling
all-nighters with friends. So why did I still feel
so far from my original expectations? Maybe it
was the fact that I hadn't fallen in love with the
whole experience– the fact that I wasn't half as
ready for the world as I thought I was. I wasn't
half the person I wanted to be. And I needed to
find a way to become that person.

I was only a few weeks in to my second
semester when I got to the breaking point and
decided to call my old high school guidance
counselor. Mary was not only my guidance
counselor but also a member of my old church.

"I just don't feel like I'm fitting in here," I told her. "Even though it's a Christian school, it feels like it's not helping my faith at all. I hardly feel any motivation to reflect Jesus when I'm just around a bunch of Christians all the time. And I don't even need to be at a Christian school now that my major is Education.... And I miss my family. I want to be closer to them. I hate not being able to go home whenever I want to...."

When I was done with my woeful rambling, she answered, "Kim, that's ok. Remember, when you decided to go to North Central, it was to try it out. Now you know that it's not what you want, and you can try something else. I'll bet you could transfer to UNR right now if you wanted to."

She had mentioned University of Nevada, Reno (UNR) to me before and I had stuck up my nose at it. Almost everyone who graduates from Lassen High School goes to UNR because it's the closest university to Susanville. Sure, Reno was a fun city to visit on the weekends, but for college, it was too close, too familiar. How lame, I'd thought. But now, the suggestion got me excited. It was perfect! It was a little over an hour away from home, so I could have my independence and dependence at the same time! Plus, the idea of getting back into public school invigorated me. Maybe that was the ticket to regaining my spiritual life– actually having people to witness to. I still had the heart of a missionary, and I was going to use it!

33

I thanked her from the bottom of my heart, and called my parents right away.

"I'm going to transfer to UNR in the fall!" I shouted excitedly to my mom, tears of joy running down my cheeks. My mom matched my hysteria and for that moment it was like there was no distance between us at all, our emotions so bridged the gap.

That moment was one of the highest points of the entire year.

**

Things were certainly looking up, and my heart felt so much lighter. I finally felt like I could make the most of my time in Minneapolis. And there was an awful lot to love. The city itself was beautiful and booming, my new friends were so much fun, and my church there beheld some of the sweetest people I've ever met.

Pastor Steve (the Associate Pastor at North Springs Church) became like a father to Kate and me. He would pick us up every Sunday and drive us the thirty-or-so miles to our church in Lino Lakes. It was a small, friendly church body, so after the services, there would be a time of fellowship and snacks in the adjoining room. Pastor Steve would always make neat little care packages to send us home with. Then he would take us out to lunch before the drive home to North Central. Between the time spent in the car and at the various restaurants, we got to know each other very well.

He was a jolly, faith-filled man but I could always sense an underlying sadness. He was now in his forties and had never been married, but you could tell his greatest desire was to be a husband and a father, and I knew he would be great at both.

Sometimes he would visit us at school to sit in on a chapel service or to have lunch with us. On one such occasion, the three of us found ourselves seated at the campus deli. He said he had something important to tell us.

He told us of his past afflictions, admitting that he'd even gotten to the point where he'd tried to take his life a few times because of the pain and abuse that he had faced.

"You guys don't know how much you encourage me," he said with red, glossy eyes. "I've undergone a lot of hurt, but God has blessed me so much with you two. I truly see you as my daughters, and that makes my heart happy."

Tears came to my own eyes. It encouraged me to know that I had helped lift the spirits of someone else, especially someone who needed and deserved it so much. There were reasons why I was at North Central, even just for a short time. This made me think maybe my relationship with David had been meant to be, too, for the time it had lasted.

Maybe God wasn't a liar.

***

35

The rest of the semester passed quickly. I hardly slept I was out so much with my friend Amy—exploring downtown, going to concerts and making new friends. I got more attached to them than I thought possible in the short time I was there.

"I'll miss you so much," I cried into Amy's arms.

"I've never had a best friend like you," Amy cried back to me.

"We'll always be friends," I replied, knowing from experience that no, it wouldn't be the same when we lived apart from each other, but yes, I would keep a place in my heart just for her.

It was equally hard to say goodbye to Pastor Steve and the other friends that I'd formed such close bonds with, but I was stronger now than I had been saying goodbye to my high school friends a year ago.

I knew what it was to live apart from people I loved, and I knew what it meant to have to make hard decisions—to let go of those who may have only been a part of my life for a season, and to hold on tight to those I really couldn't live without. I knew what it was to struggle—with love, with faith, with life passion and direction—and I knew what it was to overcome.

This had been a challenging year, but I had learned some important truths. I learned that God wasn't a liar – in fact, He was a patient,

gracious Father who saw me through my
limited thinking. I learned that "a man's heart
plans his way, but the Lord directs his steps"
(Proverbs 16:9). And I learned that the romantic
idea that people leave their parents' nests and
immediately become hip, have-it-all-together
adults is not accurate.

Which meant that I still had some learning to
do.

***

I had a high school friend named Matt who
was beginning college studies in Reno at the
same time as me, so we decided to become
roommates. We had gotten to know each other
well through youth group and he had become
like a brother to me. Over the summer, our
parents took us to tour apartments near our
respective schools, and we settled on one that
was comfortable and affordable, albeit not in
the best part of town.

Matt and I got along pretty well as
roommates but admittedly did not spend as
much time together as we had imagined. On
weeknights, Matt seemed to always want to be
out and about socializing while I was happier to
watch kid movies on my laptop after long hours
of studying and working as a preschool teacher.

On weekends, I was the absent one, always
opting to drive the hour and a half home to stay
at my parents' house rather than staying in

Reno. If you're thinking that sounds excessive, you'd be right except that my trips were not only to make up for lost time with my family after being across the country from them for a year, but also to visit with my new boyfriend.

My romance with Christopher took me by surprise. He had actually confessed his feelings for me when I had visited home from Minneapolis over Christmas break, and I had not known what to think. I had gotten my wisdom teeth removed over the break, and he was one of my most frequent visitors that would come to the house and check on me. We had known each other since junior high, and I always loved being around him because he wasn't someone you had to work to have a good time with. He seemed to enjoy himself no matter what was going on, and his silliness could always make me smile. I had always considered him to be one of the best guys I knew. He was a true gentleman, and his life emitted a joy and a gentleness that's hard to find. My sister Sandi would refer to him as "a prize trophy." She had wanted us to date since before we even met. Christopher had never had a girlfriend. He could have—I'm certain of it— but he seemed to be above the worldly drama of relationships.

Over break he had been hanging out with me quite a bit, and he came to visit late one night during my bedridden recovery, balloons in hand. He smiled nervously as he walked in and sat down beside me on my parents' living room couch. He also carried with him a stuffed pink flower. I had told him once a long time ago how I hated getting real flowers because they just die and they're a waste of money. He had remembered.

"I thought you could take this back to Minneapolis with you and remember me when you look at it," he said as he handed it to me. I smiled.

"Thank you." And then, he dove right in.

"I like you, Kim.... I really like you. You're so smart and beautiful and fun.... I don't think that now is a good time to become boyfriend and girlfriend since we live so far apart, but I just wanted to let you know how I feel.... What do you think?" he stammered.

I had no idea what to say. I couldn't believe that Christopher Darnell was that interested in me! I was certain that this was the first time he'd ever told a girl anything like this. Why was I so special? I had always thought of him as being out of my league since he was so perfect and pure. I remember having conversations with other girls from youth group, and we had all agreed that whoever was going to marry Chris would be so lucky. I had a crush on him years ago before David and I had even started dating, but I didn't know what to think of it now. We had been friends for so long that it was hard to see us as anything else.

I tried to collect my thoughts as quickly as possible. He was waiting for me to say something!

"Well... I'm flattered that you think so much of me. I mean, you're Chris Darnell," I laughed nervously. That made him happy. He took my hand in his, and we spent the rest of the night watching the movie Sweet Home Alabama. It felt like a dream.

It wasn't until Valentine's Day came around that I knew that I was falling for him. He had been calling me regularly since my visit home, and I talked to him almost every night. I enjoyed the attention and companionship but still wasn't sure if it would come to anything. On the night of Valentine's Day, we were talking as I got ready for bed and he asked if I had checked my mail that day. I said no and could immediately sense from his disappointment that there would be something waiting for me in my mailbox the next day.

I hadn't expected to be so excited, but my eyes lit up when I saw Christopher's handwriting on the package, and a giddy smile plastered itself on my face. Inside were a bunch of mini Kit Kat bars (my favorite) and a poem that Christopher had typed up on specialty paper with a border of red roses. My heart raced and my smile widened as I read the lines he'd written for me:

"I wish you were here today but it can't be that way.

Know your picture's in my mind and that it's framed and hung high."

That was the recurring line, interspersed with other rhymes that were equally romantic.

"Oh my word, that is so cute, Kim!" my friend Amy exclaimed. She had insisted on being with me when I opened the package.

"I know!" I agreed, dumbstruck. All I could do was smile and reread the poem again and again, more excitement building up the closer I analyzed the words.

"You cannot deny that you like this boy anymore!" Amy insisted. "Just look at you!"

I laughed. She was right.

***

Because we had been friends for so long, it didn't take long for my relationship with Christopher to get serious. We had only been officially dating for a few months when I told him I loved him for the first time.

It was the end of one of my weekend visits, and he was saying goodbye to me at my car before I had to drive back to Reno for the school week. I told him how hard it was to say goodbye. Even though I'd see him in five days, there was a growing longing within me to see him every day. As we hugged, I didn't want to let go and those three words just slipped out.

He didn't respond at first, and I felt my face flush as a host of emotions set in: embarrassment, confusion, sadness, even anger. If he didn't feel the same way, what was I doing spending every weekend of my time with him?

When he finally spoke, he stammered, "I.... think I love you....No, I know I love you," and gave me an even tighter embrace. All of my scattered emotions heaved a sigh of relief. I knew he had never said those words to another girl before, and they were weighty to him, not just a phrase to be thrown around. He took the time he needed to mean what he said, and it made me love him even more.

Those feelings, coupled with the fact that we were always hanging out in the evenings by ourselves, made for quite a battle with sexual temptation. Saving ourselves for marriage was a huge part of our faith, but in those moments alone together, it was difficult to keep our resolve. What started as harmless cuddling could quickly turn into touching that was inappropriate for our standards of purity. Every time we crossed a line, we would eventually get to a conversation about how we needed to pray and wait, but the more frequent those conversations became, the more disheartened I felt. Why was this so hard?

Neither of us felt like we could talk to other people about it, so we faced our struggle in solitude, not seeing a way out. Before we knew it, we had crossed the biggest line that we had never imagined we would cross. It was not deliberate. It felt more like a blur that was over before I realized what had happened. But it was an exciting blur that beckoned for our return over the next few weeks, and each time, it was a little easier to give in.

I felt overrun with guilt. Guilt which kept me spending more time trying to appear good than to actually do good. My vision of this time at UNR being my chance to reach out to others and make a difference felt unfulfilled and unattainable. I began to question where God was and why He wasn't helping me live the way He asked me to.

I wasn't the only one struggling with how to live for God during this time of life. When I was in the midst of my struggle, my roommate Matt had decided that he wanted to "take a break" from church. We were at Taco Bell for lunch one weekday afternoon when he told me. When I asked him why, he said he just wanted to.

"I'm sorry to hear that," I said. "That makes me sad."

"I don't understand why people think it's sad," he replied. "It's just not what I want to do right now."

We carried on with our lunch, but my heart felt weighed down for days to come. Surely, giving up on God wasn't the answer... or was it?

God answered in a big way one night. When I first transferred to UNR, I got plugged in to Campus Crusade for Christ, a small weekly gathering of Christian students. We would have student leaders speak on different Bible topics each meeting. To this day, I can't remember what the topic was about that night, but I can remember the one quote the speaker mentioned that spoke right from God's heart to mine: "Don't focus on what you don't understand. Focus on what you do understand and choose not to live by."

Those words floored me. I grabbed a pen and wrote them down in bold ink and didn't hear another word spoken the rest of the night. The truth was that while I didn't understand everything about God and how He works, I did understand that He was real and that He loved me. I realized that nothing could ever change those things, and that was enough for me to hold onto my faith, not just that day, but forever.

That night I went from relating to God as His child to relating to Him as his beloved.

The truth is that God has offered a better way, but there are going to be times that I don't get it and there are going to be times that other people don't get it. As I heard in another quote some time ago, the key isn't knowing all the answers, it's knowing the One who does. It may sound like a cop-out, but for me, from that day on, it makes as much sense to my brain as it does to my heart. God wants us to be close to Him, to lean on Him and rely on Him and "work out our faith," not to be able to understand and apply formulas. If everything could be grasped and foreseen, it would detract from God's relational character. And who wants to serve a God who isn't relational, one who doesn't love you and meet you even when you're wandering away?

PART III: THE LIFE

It was a late weekday night when I caught Christopher watching pornography. We had been married for three and a half years. In church I had heard that many men struggle with lust in secret but I never suspected that it was a struggle for my husband. I was wrong. Christopher routinely stayed up later than me because I always wanted to get to sleep by 10:00. He would usually be playing video games at the corner desk in our bedroom when I said good night and got into bed. I was usually a sound sleeper, but on this particular night, I woke up with the computer's light in my face and saw the image of a woman bending over and peering over her shoulder, wearing nothing but a scant G-string. I blinked hard, wondering if I was really seeing what I thought I was, when Christopher turned around and noticed that I was awake. He rushed to minimize the screen and shut down his computer while I laid there baffled, my heart and mind racing.

Christopher didn't speak as he got into bed beside me. I was laying on my side with my body turned away from him. He laid down close to me. I stiffened at his touch as he put his arm around my waist. It felt foreign and off-putting. By this point, I was wide awake, wondering what I should say or do. I'm sure he was experiencing the same thing. Finally, I broke the silence.

"What were you watching?"

He heaved a short sigh before replying, "...Porn... I was watching porn. I'm sorry."

"... Is this the first time, or do you watch it regularly?"

"No... I mean, I don't watch it every day or anything."

"How often?"

"I don't know... maybe once every couple weeks."

"For how long?"

"... A while... I'm sorry."

My voice cracked as I asked my last question. "Why?"

"... I don't know. I don't want to do it. I've stopped before... but it's hard."

I didn't know what to say, but I felt a creeping sense of panic. I excused myself to the bathroom and closed the door. The tears flowed freely now as my shock turned to grief. A million questions flooded my mind: *Why? Was I not good enough? How could he have kept such a big secret for so long? Do I even know my own husband?*

When my tears turned to loud sobs, Christopher knocked lightly and walked in to find me sitting with my head in my hands, shoulders shaking. He wrapped his arms around me and tried to calm me, telling me how sorry he was and how much he loved me. His words felt empty. *How can you love someone and be unfaithful? How can you love someone and not tell the truth?*

Eventually exhaustion set in and we returned to bed. After a few hours of tossing and turning and silently crying out to God, our alarms were already going off to wake us up for work. I had a client appointment that I felt like I couldn't miss, so I readied myself, avoiding eye contact with Christopher, still not knowing how to act toward him.

As soon as my appointment was finished that morning, I went into my supervisor's office and announced that I was going home.

"Is everything okay?" he asked.

"I'm just not feeling very good," I said honestly.

***

You may think it strange that I'm beginning this section on abundant life with a story about struggle, but if there's one thing I've learned, it's that the life Jesus gives is not about great circumstances. It's about not being alone. This story could have had a sad, dark ending if it wasn't for the relationship I had with Jesus, but because I had Him to run to, I didn't fall apart, and neither did my marriage.

When I returned home from work that day, I journaled, prayed, cried, and pleaded with my Father and Friend. Then I got on my laptop and read every Christian article I could find about what to do when your husband struggles with pornography. I researched until Christopher got home from work, and when he walked through the door, I hugged him and told him the steps that I thought were important to take: We were going to install Web protection on his computer. We were going to ask for accountability and support from our mentors at church. And most importantly, we were going to pray and believe together that God would redeem him and our marriage.

***

Reno was not the place for us. Its spiritual climate matches its desert landscapes: dry and desolate. After graduating from UNR, I had found a great job as an educational consultant, but everything else in our lives felt lacking. We didn't have very many close friends there, our marriage was in need of repair, and we were spiritually weary. I was glad when Christopher decided he wanted to study radiologic technology and look for a program out of state. We figured it would be nice to have a new beginning somewhere, and a fun adventure before we had anything tying us down to a specific place. With my recent degree, I hoped it would be easy to land a job wherever we ended up.

Between the two of us, we spent hours upon hours going through all of the certified two-year programs across the country and came up with a short list of the most affordable programs of interest. Unfortunately, it was late spring when we started looking, and we had missed many of the application deadlines for the coming fall. The only one that we could still apply to for that school year was in Tulsa, Oklahoma. Although our sole point of reference to Tulsa was that one of our favorite characters from *Friends* temporarily lived there, we decided to go for it.

The application process included an in-person interview, so we had anxiously prepared for the day that Christopher would fly out for it. It was mid-week, and I was at work checking my phone every few minutes to see if Christopher had texted any updates. The first one I received from him was on his layover in Denver.

I MISSED MY FLIGHT. WAITING IN LONG LINE TO SEE WHAT'S NEXT.

I called him at my earliest opportunity. It turned out that a flight delay had caused several people from his flight to miss their connection to Tulsa. The staff had directed them all to hurry to their gate because the plane was being held for them, but when they arrived, they were told the plane had already taken off.

Christopher waited in the long customer service line only to find out that the next flight to Tulsa wasn't for hours, so there was no way he could interview that day. The next flight home was also a ways out. He ended up spending his whole day in the Denver airport before returning home late that night. Frustrated and discouraged, he didn't even try to reschedule the interview. We would not be moving for his schooling that year.

I have never seen God's hand so clearly closing one door and opening another than in the case of where we ended up moving. At the time that Tulsa didn't work out, I knew all things happened for a reason, but I would be lying if I said I wasn't disappointed. I felt like a child that had thought recess was in just a few minutes only to realize she'd misread the clock and the long day had just started. For me, it was a long day of watching Christopher go to a monotonous warehouse job while we painstakingly researched and applied to other schools.

It wasn't until over a year later when we arrived in Huntsville, Alabama that I got a glimpse of some of God's reasons.

And they were good.

***

We arrived in Alabama with nothing but our one packed car, our dog Roxy, and a list of potential apartments we had researched online. A moving truck with all of our belongings was a few days behind us, awaiting an address to make the drop-off. We had only visited Huntsville once before, for a one-night stay a couple of months prior. As with many other radiologic technology programs, Christopher had been required to attend an in-person interview in early spring, and we had excitedly received his acceptance letter several weeks thereafter. Huntsville had been our first choice of all the programs we'd visited.

We had taken five days to drive from Reno to Huntsville. We felt like pioneers and loved spotting prairie dogs in Wyoming, rocky bluffs in Colorado, fireflies in Illinois. Even Roxy impressed us with her amiable travelling temperament. She's a Chihuahua/Miniature Pinscher mix, and the kind of little dog that will curl up in her pet bed no matter where you put it. We had a couple of sleeping bags in the backseat beside her, and every once in a while, she would climb up on top of those for a change of scenery, but she never seemed to get too restless on our long journey.

We checked into a hotel near downtown Huntsville on a Friday night. As we got ready for bed, we planned a route to check out some apartments the next day and hopefully find our new home.

With the expectation that I could find a job at a similar salary to the one I'd left behind in Reno, the budget we had set for ourselves for rent was $600 a month, and we had made our list of apartments to look at based off of that figure. We really liked the first one we visited. It was called The Reserve at Research Park and it was a big complex within minutes to each of the three major highways in Huntsville. We were surprised when the leasing agent told us the rate they could offer us was $650 even though we had seen listings as low as $580 online. She said the rates changed daily based on a program they used that tracked market values. We were hoping to find a place that day so we moved on to look at others.

We were disappointed by all of them. They were run-down, too small, had exorbitant pet fees, or were similarly asking a higher rate than they advertised online. Some didn't even have staff at the office even though their websites indicated that they were open on weekends.

Back at our hotel that evening, we decided to open our search to houses for rent on Craigslist and any other apartments we could find that were open on Sundays. We also searched online to find a church to visit. With nothing else to go off of, we Googled "non-denominational Christian church," and read a few of the belief statements of the churches in our area. We decided to try Summit Crossing Community Church because its descriptions were very thoughtful and Biblically based.

Summit was a big church in a less-than-glamorous building. No tall steeples or stained glass windows – just a plain building with such limited parking that all of the latecomers had to park on the grass hill of the fireworks shop beside it. Nonetheless, we felt very welcomed, and we loved the preaching and the worship music. They had also announced a class to get to know the church more and get involved in smaller groups that met throughout the week, so we made a mental note to attend the following Sunday.

We drove by a couple of nearby houses for rent afterward, but were again put off by one thing or another. By the end of the day, we were feeling quite discouraged. Much of our anticipation was now feeling marred by exhaustion and stress. We only had a couple of places on our list that hadn't been accessible over the weekend that might be good prospects.

We decided to call ahead from the car before we left the parking lot on Monday morning. All of our calls ended with sighs over higher costs than we felt we could manage with one income. I was starting to get frustrated and irritable before we'd even been anywhere that day.

"I'm going to call The Reserve back. Maybe their price has gone down," Christopher offered.

Yeah, right, I thought and continued looking through my apartment guide for other options as he asked the agent what the one-bedrooms were going for that day.

"$604?" I heard him say, and I looked over at him, surprised and hopeful. "Great, we're on our way!"

We signed a lease and got the keys that same day. It was just in time to tell our moving truck, which had just gotten into town, and my parents, who had travelled even further than us to help us get settled in. They had left from northern California a couple of days before us on my dad's motorcycle, and had taken their time camping at different places along the way before meeting us in Huntsville. It was the trip of a lifetime for my biker dad. My mom enjoyed herself, too, but was quite relieved to finally arrive in Huntsville. She was ready for a break from tent camping that allowed for long showers, fresh laundry, and air conditioning.

As amazingly as our apartment find was orchestrated by God, Summit Crossing Community Church was an even bigger answer to prayer. After attending the class to learn more about their beliefs, we had eagerly signed up to get connected with a missional community group, which was a smaller group of people from the church who all lived in the same part of town and were able to encourage each other and serve together throughout the week.

The group we were matched with met on Thursday nights in a house that was about three miles from our apartment. We pulled up a few minutes early the first night we attended, and I remember taking Christopher's hand and praying that we'd meet at least one couple our age that we could connect with. We had been in Huntsville for about two weeks, and now that our to-do's and time with my parents had come to an end, we were desperate to bond with people who loved the Lord, desperate to see if life here would be different than it was in Reno.

By the time the evening was over, we had met not one, but seven young couples! The entirety of our group was people in our age group that were more welcoming and friendly than either of us could have anticipated.

When we got back into our car to leave that night, we joined hands that had just hours before been anxious and pleading. Now our hearts and hands were light, and we smiled all the way home.

***

Although God had granted us a great place to live and a great church, not everything was extraordinary. I'll never forget my first birthday in Huntsville, just a week after we had moved into our new apartment. It was Christopher's first day of school, so I had dropped him off early for class and had planned to drop off resumes at some places nearby. After walking into the few offices that I thought I might have a chance at striking it lucky, I stopped at the Starbucks down the street from the hospital to get my free birthday drink.

My birthday reward at Starbucks was a simple treat that I looked forward to each year, but as I sat down with my caramel macchiato this particular Monday, I was suddenly aware of how alone I was. I had text messages from friends and family wishing me a happy birthday that initially brought a smile to my face, but by the end of reading my mom's long stream of affectionate words, I felt tears sting my eyes.

Ordinarily, I would be surrounded by friends and family at a campground at Lake Almanor. I would be eating Cinnamon Pop-Tarts and relaxing in a camp chair, perhaps readying to set up a morning board game or open some small gifts from friends. Later we would all go down to the beach with rafts and junk food and Catchphrase in hand, and spend the day in the sunshine. That night we would roast mallows around the campfire and share bad stories until we were tired and ready to bundle up in our warm sleeping bags. This was the annual tradition that—unlike free Starbucks—would not be continuing this year.

Instead I was in a new place with no familiarity, no friends, no job, and nothing to do besides cry in my coffee and be homesick and look for work (that unbeknownst to me, would take six months to find). As I texted back my thank you's for the birthday well wishes, I couldn't help but pity myself. And that was only the beginning of what very well may have been the hardest six months of my life.

***

I kept a log of all of the jobs I applied to each week. Usually it was one or two per day, but sometimes there was nothing posted that was even close to what I was looking for. Fortunately, my aunt had told me to file for unemployment, so that income kept me from taking just any job and able to search for something "in my field." My field was hard to define, though. My education classes at UNR had left me unexcited about oversized classrooms, behavior management, separation of church and state, and overemphasis on STEM education. The subject I really loved was English, so I had switched from Elementary Education to Secondary Education with a concentration on English. Then, the idea of fulfilling my practicum hours at a high school felt just as uninviting as my Global Perspectives coursework had been! When I told my Education advisor that I wasn't looking forward to going into the schools, she suggested maybe I should just pursue English rather than Education. Although it didn't give me as clear of a career track, I felt that earning a degree in any area would open lots of doors, and I might as well enjoy what I was studying. I graduated with a degree in English (Writing), but my first job out of college was coaching students and parents at the Davidson Institute for Talent Development. And my main job during college was as a Student Advising Assistant for low-income, college-bound students. Both jobs were in an office setting with a clerical component.

Most of the jobs I applied to in Huntsville were clerical. I did apply to a few jobs working with students but I was either underqualified or I was considering jobs that could not offer the hours, money, or benefits that we were going to need to support me and Christopher while he was in school full-time. So week after week, I kept my log and was always discouraged when I had to strikethrough a job that I had officially not gotten.

Just a few weeks in to my job search, I decided to post flyers at my apartment complex to offer child care, pet-sitting, and tutoring services to keep me busy in the meantime and at least earning something. This did help me land a couple of good tutoring jobs, but more frequently, I would get calls asking how much I charged that would not amount to anything. I would say, "I need to make at least $10-15 an hour," and they would say, "Well, my daycare only charges $100 for the whole week" or "Is it less for overnight care?" I would wonder if I should lower my prices or if I really had anything valuable to offer to anyone. This is the worst part of unemployment—feeling like you haven't found work because you aren't valuable. This is the big lie that God was teaching me to overcome, and not just when it came to work.

Feeling "not good enough" was also a side effect of having a husband who still continued to struggle with pornography. Every several weeks I would catch Christopher looking at something he shouldn't and once again come face to face with the question *Why?* I felt like maybe if I lost weight or dressed differently or changed my hairstyle, maybe then the problem would stop. In the meantime, I felt ugly, fat, and unloved, and each occurrence of betrayal on his part would chisel another piece off of my quickly depleting self-esteem.

The final piece came off one night in December. I had just returned home and still had my purse in hand as I noticed the inappropriate photos up on the computer screen. Christopher and I sat down next to each other on the bed as he apologized. My disappointment at the all-too-familiar confrontation suddenly turned into an escalating surge of anger. One minute I was sitting there in stony silence and the next, I was throwing my purse to the ground and screaming about how unfair this was, how I shouldn't have to feel this way. I don't think I had ever felt quite so enraged. My face was red and hot, my hands were shaking, and I fumbled over my words, my voice cracking and high-pitched.

Once I started, it was hard to stop. My pent-up stream-of-consciousness just all came out in one big ball of rage and hopelessness, that ended with a demand that we see a marriage counselor.

"Do you really think that will help?" Christopher asked. I had wondered the same thing, and also wondered how we were going to afford it with neither of us working. But the truth was I didn't know how to deal with a husband I couldn't trust, and I needed someone to show me how.

"I don't know," I said honestly, shaking my head and trying to regain my composure. "But we have to do something."

***

Counseling was not how I imagined it would be. This was probably because we had a somewhat unconventional counselor. Jeff Townsley was an older, fit gentleman with his short, grey hair combed over to the side. He wore a big, reassuring smile and fairly casual attire—slacks and a polo shirt with a leather belt fitted around his waist. We had contacted him at the recommendation of one of our church elders after the initial suggestion was way out of our price range. Jeff had such a heart for helping couples he said he was willing to meet with us for whatever we could afford.

We met for the first time in a sunny room on a December morning. Christopher and I sat nervously beside each other on a couch, and Jeff sat across from us in a chair, Bible and notepad in hand. He did his best to make us feel at ease by making small talk with us, offering us water, and making us feel more like new church acquaintances than the desperate, underpaying clients that we were. He was warm and kind. One of his first targeted questions was what our goals were. What did we hope to accomplish by the end of our time seeing him?

That was easy for me.

"I don't want my husband to look at porn anymore," I said, feeling if there was ever a time to be direct and honest, this was it. "I want to be able to trust him."

Christopher echoed my desires. Now was the part where I thought we'd delve into each of our pasts and feelings, and that very well may have been the case with a typical counselor. But Jeff Townsley lent us a Bible and had us open to the book of Ephesians. We read some verses aloud about wisdom and the Holy Spirit, and he asked us what practical truths we could apply to our everyday life. It felt more like a Bible study than a counseling session!

He also had us brainstorm the top three things that the other did well to show love and respect, as well as the top three things that we could work on. Not abstract, unhelpful things, like "love me better" but tangible things like "point out my good qualities" or "initiate Bible reading together." I realized looking at Christopher's list that this wasn't just about him changing or proving his love to me. It was an opportunity for me to prove my love to him by being willing to walk alongside him and be his helper. If I decided to choose joy and forgiveness instead of constantly nagging and complaining, it might just help both of us have a better experience in our marriage.

For homework, Jeff asked us to do two acts of kindness for each other that demonstrated our love. We were not supposed to point out what we did, and the following counseling session, we would share the things that we noticed the other person doing.

We were also to make lists of date ideas in the categories of Free, $5 dates, $10 dates, $20 dates, and $50 dates. I had always thought we were good when it came to dating because we spent quite a bit of time together, but Jeff stressed the importance of having planned dates that took place weekly. One week, I would plan a date for Christopher, and the next, he would plan one for me, and so on. The goal was not just to spend time together but to make the other person feel special with all of the creative details that you prepared for them, and to build positive memories.

I walked away from our first session feeling a lot of different things at once. Embarrassed at handing Jeff a $20 check when he clearly deserved about 5 or 6 times that amount. Confused that we hadn't talked much about our qualms. Challenged that there were some things I needed to do, too. But most of all, I felt hopeful. Although some of his ideas seemed too simple to affect much change, they gave me something positive to focus on. His style reminded me of the Bible verse "Do not be overcome by evil, but overcome evil with good" (Romans 12:21). While it seemed odd that we weren't looking back and trying to get to the root of the problem, it also felt refreshing to just look forward and see something other than disillusionment.

***

Come January, it had been six full months of job-hunting to no avail. I'd had several interviews and a couple of offers, but they couldn't provide the minimum salary I was looking for, so I'd had to turn them down. Fortunately, I made bits of cash with my neighbors at the apartment complex, either tutoring or caring for kids and pets. I'd even spent a couple of weeks doing contract secretarial work for a small law firm with hopes that it would turn into a permanent position, but that turned out to be a terrible work environment and neither me nor the lawyer was excited to pursue a long-term arrangement.

I was about to receive my last unemployment check, which meant the time had almost come for me to take whatever job I could get, rather than having the luxury of being choosy about what a suitable job would be. I had a few interviews lined up that last week of collecting unemployment, and I could only hope that one of them would work out.

When I walked in to my interview for a Secretary II position at the Alabama Institute for Deaf and Blind (AIDB), I immediately felt welcome and at ease. There was a warm, older woman who sat at the front desk and made small talk with me while I waited to be called back. The gentleman who came to lead me to the conference room was a big, smiling man with the thickest eyeglasses I'd ever seen. I would later find out that he was legally blind but had been working independently all his life,

65

just like so many of the other inspiring staff and clients at AIDB. He introduced himself as the Director of the center. The other panelists included the Director over all of the regional centers as well as a couple of other key staff who took turns asking me questions. By this time, I had undergone so many interviews that I no longer struggled with nervousness or fumbling for the right words, so I was able to respond naturally and even make them smile. At the end of the interview, I asked them to share what they liked about working at AIDB, and each of them spoke very genuinely about their positive experiences with other staff and the fulfillment gained from working on behalf of others. They also went over the great healthcare and vacation benefits.

"Well I hope I've made you as excited about me as you've made me about working here!" Those were some of my final words as I exited the building, with a sense that it had gone very well.

Sure enough, just a couple of days later, I got a phone call asking if I could start on Monday. Not for the bear minimum salary requirement I had set, either, but for a little more! One of the best parts was that this job was just down the street from the hospital where Christopher went to school each day, and our hours aligned perfectly for carpooling, so we wouldn't even need to take on the extra expense of another vehicle!

I felt such a wave of relief, gratitude, and awe in that moment, and even as I recount it. It had been such a hard six months of battling self-doubt and insecurity, but God had proven himself faithful. Not only as my provider but as a patient, loving teacher who wanted me to really know in my heart of hearts that my identity was not based on what I did for a living. My identity also wasn't based on how my marriage was going. Even at my worst, my identity was always the same: a beloved child of God.

***

If there's one thing I learned about God's plan for me to have an abundant life even in times of trial, it was that His family was a big part of it. The missional community group (MCG) of young couples we had joined was there week by week to pray for us, encourage us, and keep us focused on God and other people. When one of us was moving apartments or houses, we would all gather to load and haul boxes. When someone's neighbor needed help with yard work, we would come together as a team to bless them. When someone got a job or passed a test, we would celebrate with homemade desserts and cards. When Christopher and I didn't have family nearby to celebrate holidays with, we were invited to someone else's family gathering. I had seen God give me family away from home during my time in Minneapolis, but I experienced it at a whole new level with my MCG.

I had to learn to be vulnerable with them, and it did not come naturally to me. I had always maintained an image as someone who had it all together, and while it was easy to share my need for a job, it was much harder to open up to others about my marital and personal struggles. But in that familial environment, I felt the freedom and desire to be real with people in a new way. I will never forget how freeing it was the night that I let myself cry to a few of the girls and let them know how much I struggled with insecurity. I wasn't ready to tell anyone that it stemmed from Christopher's struggle with pornography, but I was ready to tell them that I felt like a mess inside and I needed their encouragement. Those girls' affirmations and prayers were like a salve that loosened the grip of brokenness I felt choking me. From that day forward, I felt a growing peace about who I was, and the comfort of knowing that if and when I forgot, I had people I could rely on to point me back to hope and truth.

My MCG not only knew how to love me well through the tears, but also through the celebrations. After hearing how terrible my first birthday in Huntsville was, they threw a "K" party just for me where everyone dressed up as something that started with the letter "K," and there were all sorts of my favorite foods, including silly menu items like a huge cookie in the shape of a K and banana pudding that had been labeled "K (potassium) pudding."

That is just one of many examples of the love and generosity that were poured out on us and steered us from living a detached life in which we could only see ourselves and our problems. Our MCG helped us find joy in realizing that life was not all about us and that it was such a blessing to be a part of a Christ-centered community.

***

We had been in Huntsville for about a year and in counseling for about seven months when the time came for us to celebrate our five year wedding anniversary. For me, this felt like the perfect opportunity for a new start, a time where we could really let go of all of the weight of our first years of marriage and reaffirm our commitment to each other. I had originally seen our move to Huntsville as that new beginning and had felt crushed when it didn't feel like anything got better. But now we were not only in a fresh landscape but had fresh vision. Counseling, community life, and the passing time and struggles had deepened our faith and our understanding of what marriage was.

I told Christopher I wanted to renew our vows. At first, I envisioned a few people there with us, but Christopher was reluctant.

Vulnerability was new for both of us, and while we had been somewhat open with our closest friends, our moment of re-dedication felt like too personal of an experience to share. We eventually decided it was just going to be between us and God. We would write our own vows and recite them to each other, just as we had for our wedding day years ago.

We booked a vacation home rental on the shoreline of the Tennessee River and stayed there for two nights. We were over 30 minutes from Chattanooga, where we did spend some time over the course of the weekend, but my favorite times were the moments sitting on the porch, cuddled in our room, or floating together in the canoe that the property owners were kind enough to let us use.

For our vow renewals, we walked down the dock hand in hand to the edge of the pier. The sun shone down on us as we took turns reading the words we had prepared for each other. Our original wedding vows had mainly been about how great we thought the other person was, and while they did express a commitment to love each other through ups and downs, those realities were so obscure and foreign then. Five years in, there were still many more harsh realities and beautiful surprises to discover, but we knew now what it meant to face real trials and stay by each other's side. So these vows were about commitment and grace and choosing a love that runs deeper than romance, a love that only God could sustain. Tears rolled down my cheeks as I read my vows to Christopher and as I heard his vows for me, and afterward we embraced and prayed together. We also took some photos to remember the occasion. I may not have been in a gown that cost several hundred dollars or surrounded by family, but the memories of that day are just as beautiful to me.

I didn't walk away with the notion that everything was going to be a fairy tale after that day. I knew we would continue to face hardships and fight the ugliness that lies inside each one of us, but I also knew that with the Lord and willing hearts, our love really could face anything and overcome.

***

We continued to thrive in Huntsville. Christopher finished his two-year program in June 2015 and got hired as a radiologic technologist just weeks later. Although it started off as part-time work, it would eventually become his first full-time position with benefits. While we had initially seen ourselves moving back to the west coast after his schooling was complete, we now felt no urgency to return. We had built a life that we loved. From the lightning bugs and lush green foliage to our church family and neighbors to our jobs and regular activities, Huntsville had become our happy place.

Our missional community continued to be a huge part of that happiness, and we faced a big hardship the day it came for us to "multiply," or break up into two smaller groups. After meeting together for a couple of years, we had grown to about 30 people, which was too many of us to keep a deep level of intimacy and discipleship or to allow for more people to be involved. This is something our church considers good news and plans for, but it is also very difficult to say goodbye to those you have been walking alongside for an extended time.

We would no longer be in a group with several of the couples we had been closest with, and my first reaction was sorrow. I didn't want to drift apart from the people that had poured so much into our lives. They had helped us learn our identity in Christ's grace and had shown us the beauty of spiritual friendship. Although we weren't relocating, the turmoil felt just as real as it did when I said goodbye to loved ones when I moved from Minneapolis.

Still, a small part of me understood that we were now being called to pour into others, to pass on the gift that we'd been given. Plus, it wasn't as if I wouldn't have any relationship with these sweet couples I was no longer seeing as regularly. Slowly, God helped me come to terms with the fact that it wasn't just about me and what I thought I wanted or needed. It was about knowing and spreading His love. And I could do that from any locale, any community, and any life circumstance. If we were to move from Huntsville or from dear friends or from a happy season to a harsh one, God would always be with me, and that would always be more than enough.

***

That harsh season showed up just months after we'd celebrated our 7-year anniversary. We had decided to start trying to have a baby that August and were delighted when we already had a positive pregnancy test in October. We went to see the doctor right away, and at just six weeks along, we saw a throbbing heartbeat on the ultrasound screen that had us giddy with excitement. Although we wanted to tell the world, we had had some spotting and felt faintly cautious when the staff asked us to come back in two weeks for another ultrasound.

The weekend before my Tuesday appointment, I started bleeding as though I was on my period. I hoped and prayed it would subside, but I was really worried come Monday morning and called my doctor's office first thing. The nurse practitioner was very matter of fact.

"You could just be spotting, or you could be starting to miscarry," she explained. "If you'd like to come in earlier tomorrow, we can see you first thing."

Unfortunately, I had a work engagement scheduled out of town in the morning so I kept my regular afternoon appointment time. One of my coworkers looked at me that day and flat out asked me if I was pregnant. I had no idea what to say. I knew something was wrong, but I was asking God for a miracle. It had been no secret that we were trying, so I responded with something along the lines of, "You never know," and tried to change the subject. I maintained a professional composure all day, although all I could think about was what my ultrasound would show.

When I finally arrived at my appointment, I managed to keep all my wits about me until the ultrasound technician started probing me. She was not the same woman who had taken my first ultrasound, but she seemed to be just as kindhearted. There was a big screen to the right that showed me what she was seeing. Although I was laying down, my body was rigid as my eyes anxiously swept over the screen. She kept pushing the wand in different directions to move closer and get different angles. At a typical 8 week ultrasound, it should have been no problem to confirm that there was a heartbeat and that the embryo was a typical size, but in my case, there was no longer a heartbeat to be found, and there had been no growth since the last ultrasound two weeks prior. Before she said a word, I knew that I had lost my baby, and silent tears ran down the right side of my face.

"I'm sorry I don't have better news for you," she said, and commented on how a lot of women have miscarriages, often their first, but the next time they get pregnant, they have a healthy baby. I could only nod my head as I sat up. I think I managed a thank you through my tears, but when she left the room for me to get dressed, I could not contain the rush of tears and sobs that came out of me. I tilted my head back and tried to take slow, deep breaths. Finding the tissue box in the room, I cleared my nose and face a couple of times, only to have to do it again a moment later when I couldn't stop the tears from continuing. Finally, I was able to move to the room where I could visit with my doctor.

As I waited, I saw a text from Christopher asking how the appointment was going. I didn't have the words to say, so I just sent back a crying emoji face. I probably should have waited to tell him in person, but I also knew how badly he wanted to know what was happening.

My doctor sat with me through several tears and questions as we discussed what to do next. I could allow the baby to pass naturally, but that could take several days and be pretty painful, or I could schedule a D&C where they would surgically remove the tissues. I had no idea what I wanted and told her I'd call her back after talking to Christopher.

"This may be a dumb question," I asked near the end of our time together, "but is there any chance..." my words trailed off.

"In a case like this where there is a heartbeat and then there isn't, it's pretty clear that the life is gone," she said slowly. "You don't have to worry that you're aborting if you go through with the D&C." For some reason, even though I knew the truth, I needed to hear it stated that plainly for me to start to accept it.

We had planned to go to our best friends' house that night for dinner and games, so I knew I needed to call Devon on my way home and let her know what had happened. They had miscarried themselves several months earlier and had been very open with our missional community about it, so I knew she would understand what I was feeling.

"We can do whatever you want us to do," she said. "If you want to come over and talk about it, we can do that, or if you want to be distracted, we can not talk about it and just play games, or we can postpone to another night." Again, I had no idea what I wanted, so I told her I'd text her after talking to Christopher.

I arrived home before he did. All I could think to do was sit and cry and pet Roxy. When Christopher got home, he hugged me for a long time and let me cry into his shoulder and choke out all of the details and all of the questions we were supposed to have answers to. He was leaving it up to me just like everyone else.

So I made the hard decisions. I stayed home. I texted friends and family to tell them the bad news. I got a D&C and allowed friends to deliver meals over the weekend. I forced myself to talk and pray about it with Christopher and Devon and others, even though I was tempted to keep everything inside. I wrote a goodbye letter and asked Christopher to write one, too, and we folded them around our ultrasound pictures and placed them in a box that we would keep in the closet. I went to Thanksgiving and Christmas gatherings and allowed myself to cry en route. I studied about Heaven and asked God whether my unborn baby would be there. I told our missional community group. I even told a stranger: A neighbor mentioned that she was taking a girl from her church to the hospital because she'd lost her baby. I felt an immediate connection to this girl I didn't know, and I wrote her a card to let her know my experience and that I was praying for her.

There was a lingering hollowness I'd never felt before, a sense that everything was meaningless, as the writer of Ecclesiastes articulates. I went to and from work, saw friends, did chores, as I always had, but with a new ache to feel that any of it mattered.

One Thursday night, several weeks after our loss, Christopher gave his testimony at missional community group. At this point we were now co-leading the group after another multiplication and were still in the formative time of trying to establish depth with one another. I watched my husband speak openly about his struggles and how God had been faithful to renew his heart. I saw the people around listen to a leader who wasn't ashamed to be open and vulnerable about his imperfection and his need for Jesus, and a thought of hope landed in my mind: *This* is meaningful. That God had brought us through so much, and even in the midst of grief, we could proclaim God's faithfulness. That we could bring hope to others who also struggled with sin and doubt and the weight of this world. That we could unashamedly own up to our brokenness and point to a Savior who truly redeems.

***

As the new year began, I sensed a new chapter beginning in my life as I turned the page on grief. Though the heartache was far from over, it was less heavy, and Christopher and I decided to start trying again. We took our first pregnancy test in January. When we saw the negative sign, there was a slight disappointment, but I felt God calling me to contentment in my current circumstances. I had a loving husband, a wonderful support network, a great workplace, and a thriving missional community— my blessings were many! There was also a reminder not to rush the current season I was in to get to the next one. I had hope that a baby was in our future, but I asked God for grace to enjoy the present.

As a Valentine's gift to Christopher, I asked Devon to take some family photos. Just me,

Christopher, and Roxy. The thought crossed my mind before arriving to the photo shoot that if things had progressed normally with our pregnancy, then maybe we would have been taking maternity photos that day. But in the midst of the sadness that thought beckoned, there was a deep joy that allowed my heart to truly celebrate life and my family just the way it was. What a sweet season it was to get to enjoy each other and grow together, spoil our only dog, and share our lives with so many wonderful people.

We took a pregnancy test later that week and were elated to see a positive result! I thought to myself, *Isn't it just like God to have given me a "maternity" shoot even when I didn't know it?*

And that same God also gave us another dog and our first house in the next two months. My season of sorrow had quickly become a season of celebration.

Now I write with squirming, growing life inside of me, and I reflect on how truly blessed my life is. I've asked myself if I were to lose this baby, what would happen to my faith then? What about my husband, or my job?

I feel I can say with confidence now having wrestled with a fragile marriage and joblessness and loss, that I would still have abundant life. I don't know what's to come, and I still haven't figured out my unique missional path, but I'm confident God will use me to make an impact on the people around me. No matter what,

God's love and hope are as real and as near as the kicks I can feel within me.

Jesus has not only called me His child and his beloved, but also His friend. I'm someone He comforts in times of hardship, celebrates with in times of joy, and strengthens in times others need grace. We take delight in knowing each other and walking together through it all.

And isn't that the life?

AFTERWORD

God redeems. At the time of publication, my dad has been sober from alcohol for over 15 years, and Christopher has been living in freedom from pornography for several months. We gave birth to a healthy son, Noah Gabriel. Noah means "comfort and rest" and Gabriel means "The Lord is my strength," so his name is a constant reminder for my striving heart.

I wrestled with God about sharing my story for a long time, wanting to keep my struggles hidden and keep up the goody two-shoes image that I started building way back in childhood. It's not until the last few years that I've learned that it truly benefits no one to act like I have it all together. What the world needs to hear is that my life is not perfect, and that I have not earned good standing with God. I used to think I had to, but the beautiful truth of the gospel is that I don't, I can't, and there's no need to because Jesus already earned it in my place! My hope is not in a perfect life here on this earth, or in my own righteousness. My hope is that Jesus has saved, is saving, and will save me from the brokenness within and around me.

As you put this book down, I hope it's this good news that leaves a lasting impression on your heart. Jesus is the way, the truth, and the life!

ACKNOWLEDGMENTS

All glory be to God, both for my actual life events and for the making and publishing of this book. He is the only reason you're reading this! My pride lost to His Spirit's prompting.

To Christopher and my other family and friends who were featured in my story, thank you for your bravery and willingness to share even the unflattering details. You inspire me to do the same.

To Devon, for lending your talents and time as a photographer and cover designer, but even more so for your support in reading, praying, encouraging, and helping me in any way you could. I couldn't have done it without you!

To my fellow writers from Huntsville Writer's Group, thank you for your critiques on hard subject matter, and for spurring me on to keep writing.

To my support team of friends, family, teachers, mentors, and other loved ones, thank you. I am honored you took the time to read my story, affirm it, review it, promote it, and all of the other little things in between.

Join my email list to STAY IN TOUCH and
receive a FREE PDF of Questions for Reflection!

https://mailchi.mp/4ad9d5f2280d/kimdarnell

Made in the USA
Columbia, SC
10 January 2020